Darklight

Also by Toby Olson:

Poetry

Human Nature
Unfinished Building
We Are the Fire
Sitting in Gusevik
Still / Quiet
Two Standards
Birdsongs
The Florence Poems
Aesthetics
Doctor Miriam
Three & One
Home
Changing Appearances
City
The Wrestlers & Other Poems
Fishing
Vectors
Pig/s Book
The Hawk-Foot Poems
Worms into Nails
Maps

Fiction

The Bitter Half
The Blond Box
Write Letter to Billy
At Sea
Reading
The Pool
Dorit in Lesbos
Utah
The Woman Who Escaped from Shame
Seaview
The Life of Jesus

Darklight

Toby Olson

Shearsman Books
Exeter

First published in the United Kingdom in 2007 by
Shearsman Books Ltd
58 Velwell Road
Exeter EX4 4LD

www.shearsman.com

ISBN-13 978-1-905700-23-3

ISBN-10 1-905700-23-7

Copyright © Toby Olson, 2007.

The right of Toby Olson to be identified as the author of this work has been asserted by him in accordance with the Copyrights, Designs and Patents Act of 1988. All rights reserved. No part of this publication may be reproduced, stored in a retrieval system, transmitted in any form or by any means, electronic, mechanical, photocopying, recording or otherwise, without the prior permission of the publisher.

Acknowledgements
Some of these poems have appeared in the following magazines: *Colorado Review, Conjunctions, Denver Quarterly, Golden Handcuffs, Mulberry Anthology* and *New American Writing*. The fourteen poems of 'My Little Plane' were originally composed to accompany a series of aerial photographs made by the artist Diane Burko. In that context, the poems were printed below the title 'The Shadow Under the Shadow.' 'Reversal of Fortunes' was published in *The PIP Gertrude Stein Awards For Innovative Poetry in English 2005-2006* (ed. Douglas Messerli, Green Integer, Los Angeles / Copenhagen, 2007).

The publisher gratefully acknowledges financial assistance from
Arts Council England.

for Miriam

Contents

Darklight	9
Hesitation Waltz	11
Swiss Miss	18
Dream	22
Calaca	24
Prayer of Initiation	30
Accident of the Axe	32
At Some Time	34
Theatrical Story	40
Standard-16, I Remember You	41
Six Short Poems	48
Border Towns	52
Reversal Of Fortunes	56
That's a Thought	61
Gallery	65
Dolls	69
Prayer to the Most Powerful Hand	70
A Cole Porter Medley	72
Too Late Now	74
My Little Plane	77
Roughly There	84
Two Drunks	91
Lockout	92
Cairo	94
Foolish Heart	101
Standard-17, Some Other Time	104
Feather	111
Hooked	113
Table	114
Prayer for Travelers	119
Moon	121
Gardening	122

Darklight

Darklight above the doorway
in both X-ray and photography . . .

but not the deep significance this time
or the surface

which vibrates in the eternal present.
It's the way of the world seen

and the one apprehended, blue moon
in a haze of yellow

[she was older than she was in reality,
the fire in the hearth had died away]

though on some days
there's a certain clarity of light.

I fear this kind of thing increases
as time goes by,

though it's not exactly like that,
maybe sad sack's meanderings, half blind.

And I think this means the end is coming
before too long. If it is possible

I will miss you. In the meantime
perhaps this undeveloped deep

in dated chemical's reaction
can rise to the surface

and also be interesting,
as delicate and sentimental.

I could ride forth on a pale horse
called Dark Lantern

whose light can be blocked off
as by a sliding panel.

Hesitation Waltz

Returned again to find that spot
      where I had rested. It was gone
or changed utterly, so that I could not sit
as pivot for consideration
      nor find comfort in standing
above the spot.

All this had been mine: window, table
and chair, that illusion
      of a virgin's intensity in seeing
each beloved distinctly,
the objective world.

A tube driven into a congested throat,
      the withdrawal of a cannula
for breathing, that moment,
then a jay's cry
      called song
which is made light of in poetry,
but is lighter than that.

Here's that rainy day,
      its first word, "maybe,"
held in Bill Evans' fingers for exhaustion
of what might have been,
or a big band rendering
of *Sentimental Journey*,
a medley,
blame it on my youth, so
sweet and lovely.

Once came to a place heady
with possibilities of tempo,
was crazy for intricate figures

in the cowboy squares.
        That was dancing, fleetingly,
like the memory
of freestyle later,
     an Arizona stumblebum.
What is revealed, but such hesitations
as we go down?

Yet it's still early May, clatter
     of wet chickadees insistent
pin points of black-cap on the pine's needles
        (be then
joyful?),
dissonant melodies over block chords,
a red sail in the damp distance,
     considerations of tables and chairs.
I can't get started.

Rivers of memory, sea of memory, rainy ripples
     on a golden pond, notoriously placid
and temporary, before the arrival
     of the actors
and strife.
It's come from the desert of my boyhood
in some fashion. That boat.

     These are the pines grown into a screen
at the pond's brink.
     This is automatic writing.
The trees cry out
as the axe enters the forest,
     "Look at the handle,
he's one of us!"
I could have discovered

        that note thrown on the kitchen table,
but for the boy
            wobbly now at the gunnels
near the axe handle tiller;
he's fighting
the red sail and adolescence.
    "I'm leaving": her words
fluttering to linoleum in a household breeze.
I can see them,
in the mind's eye, through the window.

Once came in dreaming to the pond's brink.
    Once saw a girl's undergarments
in her spinning in a cowboy square.
        I was hesitant: *blame it on my youth.*
The pond was placid
in a river cast down by the moon.
    I could see the red sail, that bloody rag
of adolescence.

Watching a girl's undergarments in the mind's eye,
        no more than a stable speck in this imagination.
Yet it's still early May.
Dissonant candles
    shake like awkward dancers
in the cowboy squares,
        my sentimental journey.
I should light them at the tips
as we go down
into a moon river at this window.

Repeated figures of the dance, actual
    in the memory: cowboys looping
near a flash of undergarments

           below crinoline,
notes spilling
to a wash of sawdust near a household table,
"I'm leaving,"
gone into the death that is memory
           of a boy's boat under red sail
at the pond's iris, her face
       then rising like the moon itself
through seaweed.

This is the danger zone of the virgin.
This is automatic writing.
     These are the spot's projections
on the pond's moonglow surface,
        a carousel of shadowy faces,
my dream girls, under glass.

Yet in this rain, old interlude, other
seeds germinate invisibly
     in that sodden garden, awaiting
the new chicken-wire fence
and rabbits, some wholesomeness
of hard work
         beyond thoughts of dream girls
as women,
     or a few popular tunes: *slowpoke,*
heart of my heart, red roses
for a blue lady,
       hesitant *deep purple*
in a cowboy waltz tempo.

The cardinals have arrived,
     their insouciant arrogance tentative
in first flowers wavering

           on delicate green stalks, daffodils
heavy in a freight of rain, goldfinch,
red red robin,
a mix of wild bird seed in the rickety feeders,
    that geometric pattern
of quick chickadees lifting
        some invisible net of crinoline,
gold spun, and the weaving traces
of my neighbor's
black cat through hay.

It's early May too in that distant desert:
    what buds, what boy? Each memory
only a fake of hesitant music,
be it squares
    or the bright blindness of *moonglow*.
This is automatic writing,
    "as the axe enters the forest."
Try to forget it, in this
burgeoning.

    But we were dancing, or she was
spinning alone on her own spot, elsewhere
    and ecstatic,
within that isolate figure,
one of many,
characteristic of a cowboy square,
    unaware of those spectator figures,
        to the far corners of the hall
and the one rocking us gently,
    that childish wrangler and his allemande girl,
the hum of the world turning
under the sawing fiddles and guitars.

We fumbled around in our bodies,
        got crazy over supposed slights
and adulteries.
               We went to the movies
for those common agonies,
        traded a few awkward kisses
                in a dark alcove in Tucson
that time we drove there for a school concert
in your mother's car.
Even then,
given such virginal passions,
this was not exactly clear.

I remember the ice-cream cones,
        at Castle Rock below Copper Man.
It was early spring
and sundown:
             your eyes, your face!
We licked our chops,
at the taste. *That* was sweet.

There was even a boat with a red sail,
        a boy in shadow at the tiller
on a pond in desert oasis,
Saint David,
             not exactly golden
but still water
fed from a deep wellspring, no pines,
but willows at the brink.

        "I'm leaving," going off to Texas
for another teen life.
             The tiller wobbles

under his hand in a quick breeze.
Enter the axe.

I'm through with love
           (for a little while
at least).

All this is part
of the disposition of the figures in the dance,
     though they are not actors,
so long as acts of memory
         are discounted,
as well as an old man's garrulous
enthusiasms
in searching elsewhere for his spot.

     Beyond the window now,
in fog and rain,
the sun sets this evening like clockwork,
a common perception
recently.

     And if the world doesn't hum
in its turning, I seem to
and imagine
that pine, skeletal
         in slow advancing,
as it fades back into shadow
and the axe flashes
     at the pond's brink. Here it comes.
It is one of us.

Swiss Miss

Lingers now in peace upon the swollen tide,
ruby-throat fallen from sky in the last few hours.
This information: unblemished, on her good side,
not sleeping, and Swiss birds won't eat thistle.

After the circus and before investigation,
the fliers linger on imagination, the Bohemian
Waxwing juggler, those quick Chickadee tumblers.
The Swiss detective wears wingtips.

Lisalot, I miss you, I didn't mean to release you.
Flights of fancy and flocking in the banquet hall,
while the river, beyond filmy curtains and balcony,
runs to the lake, carrying her body as if sleeping.

Ladies and gentlemen, if you will please quit chattering,
if you will just try hard to remember, the details,
anything in the recent past. It shouldn't be difficult.
Time was I loved you, dear Lisalot, I never dropped you.

Check everyone's wrists, the nature of their shoes and
identification. Is there residual powder in anyone's palms?
Check times of arrival, those missing, each performer.
Remember, Swiss birds won't eat thistle.

Was it the proud German, Finch? That week in Luzern?
You flew as a hummingbird from the bar then, in Bern.
And check also the Limmat River, send in the clowns.
Embraceable you, sweet ruby-throat, I've washed my hands.

Feathered boas and short tights in the banquet hall,
Madam Vireo, the contortionist, and her dwarf entourage.
Check for splinters, look most carefully under the nails.
Lisalot: tossed high up in the contest in St. Gallen.

We were the rage of the competition, the odd birds
who flew out in our nature and faked danger theatrically
after those months of practice, home in Furna. I never
looked at you closely, gripping your ankles, in that way.

Then the German, Finch. Or was it that Harlequin, Jaeger?
Take but a moment to consider, Swiss birds won't eat thistle,
then take each one into a room, backstage, and ask questions.
Lisalot, my darling partner, little Swiss Miss, I warned you.

[General atmosphere: the river, ominous mist over the lake,
the Swiss detective, maybe elaborate cages hung in the hall.
He could be innocent, an accident. She could be a strumpet.
His hands, or he stands at the rear of the line murmuring.]

Please stop chattering. Defend your heads against the cages.
Prepare, please, your stage and real names and associations.
Have you been with the circus long? How well did you know
Lisalot? Things like that. What can you tell me about thistle?

Then, in Grindelwald, we were eager. The Eiger rose majestic
above the chalet, your hair silk feathers in my fingers.
Lisalot, you called my nose a beak, humming softly in laughter.
Almost love birds in an alpine cage! What becomes of me now?

A dwarf stands upon the shoulders of the Strong Man, Hawk.
His real name is Meadowlark and it's taking far too long.
He opens a few cages. Pandemonium! The fledglings can't
fly well, and feathers and death squawks flood the Hall.

[I too have been crazy in jealousy. Our cat, Flicker,
and the foreign sock he discovered under our bed.
I wanted to kill you, quite seriously, or myself then.
You, strumpet; I the virtuous dove, already in mourning.]

Attention, please. Attention! Can you please settle down?
Lunch is on the way. We'll be serving thistle today . . .
That's right, it's a joke. It's seed salad, and flesh
for those inclined. Thank you for your attention anyway.

Lisalot, Finch or Jaeger, it doesn't matter; even exotic
Bachman, warbling MC, whose song might have seduced you.
Just as I was beginning to touch you, take you under my wing.
Better had you avoided hunger, throat swelling with thistle.

Be sure, now, to check the empty cages, secreted places,
keep an eye on the ground feeders, as well as flycatchers.
Close all the windows. The ones under suspicion might
seem without guile. Clearly, this was a crime of passion.

Thistle: in his pockets, in his cuffs, in his hair; also
there is thistle in the matting over muscle on his arms.
I smell thistle! It's our detective, perky as a sparrow.
Thistle's stuck in ducts, visible at the corners of his eyes.

[I too have wept around thorns, stuck in rageful weeping.
Somehow love is indecent, if ethical considerations apply.
Yet the moves of your glorious legs. I can't describe them,
but in metaphor: legs of a hawk hanging down at landing.]

Okay, I killed you, thistle in the muesli. I'm sorry.
The last thing I wanted to do, etcetera. It was a mistake,
but I am not innocent. Lisalot, even if a dozen young men
had slept with you, even then I would still love you.

From the dead: Fuck you! I was no willing object of such
sentimental crap. I had my own agenda, and you killed me.
Christ, is it gentle here on the waves, almost exquisite,
to sleep deep on my side upon water, no man beside me.

Please behave yourselves. Miss Pelican, stop with the soaring.
The line grows shorter, and I grow increasingly satisfied.
Miss Pelican! It's a long way yet to Tipperary, but one bird
ate thistle, and thistle hangs around. Miss Swan, that's enough!

Lisalot! Your body turning cartwheels in the air, blah, blah,
your orchestrated clothing, tights forcing men into despair.
Your hair: innocent as chick-down or a diaper, blah, blah.
What can I say now? I still love you. I offer the proof.

[Your orchestrated clothing to say, I am here, look at me.
Perhaps love of necessity contains jealousy. I told you to go,
go, get out of here, only because you slept with another.
This is not love, but hypocrisy. Let me die in your arms.]

Difficulties among flycatchers, high wire and trapeze.
Count Scissortail comes to blows with a certain Phoebe,
a ruckus about relatives and partners. Madam Vireo is miffed,
sends out her dwarfs. The detective calls once again for order.

Quick as water up from the well in Furna, my sister,
news of incest on the high wire throughout the village.
It never happened. Check the quieter Towhees, their feathers.
Lisalot, each gesture, each flight, each time I caught you.

[Atmosphere: the hall a complete mess, feathers and blood,
empty as this apartment, the fled nest, no Lisalot, no you.
Thistle weighs him down, a loadstone, as much as absence
pricks like needles in our pillows, my clothing, this chair.]

You're next, last in line. Raise your arms. Wait! Where
are you going? Come back! Check the curtains, the balcony!
[Beware of extremity, hopeless desperation, and suicide.]
Then check the river for her brother, Pigeon, no kingfisher.

Dream

Dreamed of a woman lonely in a country house,
a married woman, younger than I,
with no children. It was not her dream,
though she was standing at a window
romantically in yearning. There was faint light
on a table, her form provocative in shadow.

Perhaps she was waiting for her husband
instead of me. It doesn't matter, for it was not
his dream, though he might have been thinking
carefully about her. Not really a dream,
rather a thought provoking nightmare,
since she was lonely and I was not yet there.

Dreams that are manageable, like this one,
are not dreams at all. One thinks of glory,
the passions of a savior, complete control.
She was waiting for someone approaching
on a white horse? in a cab? after a spring rain,
cuffs dampened, unruly hair, that kind of thing.

Perhaps dreaming, her eyes pass over the porch,
alight on the circular wishing-well in the garden
her husband has carefully tended, wending his way
among tender shoots, thinking of children.
Birds call. Little spring rabbits appear.
I have the answer, the key, the disruptive solution.

There is time now for the sun and the music,
for fairy-tale children dancing around the well.
There might have been time for his returning,
but this is nightmare, clouds come in, and it begins
to rain again. I might have been out there, hesitant,
under the wet young leaves of the tender oaks.

Time enough for dreaming, a dream that is not one.
Has she taken a tranquilizer, to wend herself away
from barrenness? There is time left for wishing,
but the well is a fake one, cheap, and poorly assembled.
Her husband spends time in a bar among lascivious women.
I am not sure if I am him or the fairy-tale children.

Calaca

Mystery of the unlikely, a ghost story,
but this is after the tale
    began in death and decay,
but not death,
for peonies grew from the skull's eyes,
defying that gravity
    where flesh fell, after it had risen
back to the earth's surface in hurricane,
that clear spring afternoon
    when he had leaned down
over bone, the universal visage now.
Alas, poor Madeline!

[The nose grows larger, relative
to weight loss and the shrinking flesh,
then lastly
    the nose itself falls away,
no more to be lifted
in gesture of offence taken
    nor flared out at the nostrils
in the throes of passion. 'Throes"?
    I was almost gone away
at those times,
throwing myself away.]

Before the hurricane, back pedaling, before
offense taken
    as the doctor inserted the canula,
before these material changes
    it seemed better
to move on the earth politically,
    though eventually caught that way
in criminal secrets revealed
to the far corners of the village.

[And the teeth!
What burdens are set aside
when hair falls down at the crown?
    Living by the skin of them, a skull fracture
knocking some sense in.
       To be excused,
to run on counter to expressed wishes.
I was full of myself
    those times, myself
not full of me.]

Before the reversal of fortune and the hurricane,
before night was day and Madeline the calaca,
    before light in the head lamp of the doctor,
all seemed well in the seaside village,
their serious lives,
    that comedy of complete wastefulness
celebrated.

Madeline:
cooking and cleaning, sewing,
    shopping for dinner and his comfort,
doing a little ironing, at mid-day
in the kitchen,
a focus of soreness below the clavicle.

He brought in money
and a certain perfected oblivion.
She was a dancer
       for joy and not money,
in a previous life clearly remembered.
A bell played at the gate
upon his arrival, each evening,
before day was night

      and the doctor,
there
in the throes of political passion
and the sweet presences
of the here and now.

[Brewed cups of eroded memory,
      caldron of the catalytic world. I drink
from a dipper,
flesh hangs down in the gravity,
      and the feet! and the grinding ratchet
in the shoulder!
      Were it your slipper, young
and vibrant before hurricane.
The hair falls out at the crown.]

Before the hurricane and the buildings toppled,
the madonna Madeline sits at the window
      a vision of satisfaction
when looking in.
Looking out, there's a vibrant commerce,
      the real world.
A bell plays at the gate.
She's fallen dead at the window,
just sixty-two.

[Yesterday,
stupidity of lost opportunity.
      The flesh hangs slack at the throat,
a groaning when turning
in the empty bed. And the knees,
      filaments clouding the right eye.
Who is the one left to be following?
Drink deep from the dipper.

Mystery of the unlikely, a ghost story.
Were it your slipper.]

Posada rendered the personalities of the calaveras,
        and this is becoming a village full of them,
skeletons in the streets and parks,
a number present, always, at public gatherings
and the ones arriving by boat, caught up
        in hurricane and shipwreck,
who now build a bonfire on the beach
for singing, eating, and dancing
below the rocky cliffs.

He was a politician, caught out for vote selling.
Poor Madeline. He can see her
        through the window now,
the calaca,
that parody of himself reclaiming
his reputation and stature.
        She's calling out to the gathering
wearing his clothing,
suit, *sombrero* and tie.
        Symbols of words vomit in the bone faces
of the calaveras, her jaw clacking
to convince the populace.

        And the story might end here, a lesson,
but you know, he too the skeleton
        after hurricane and resurrection
and the dancer, Madeline
assuming that ethical self he had forgotten
even in sustenance from the dipper.
He fell down dead at the window.

[Yet I am still in love!]

He, now, the calaca,
cooking and cleaning, wearing a dress
and her slippers,
waiting for bells at the gate,
but in a parody of waiting for domesticity
    possible only in gestures
        of the unexpressive skull.
Though criminal,
    yet he is at peace and happy,
if such can be said of calacas,
here in a paradise
paid for in lost stature
in the other.
        He's sitting at the window, sewing,
while outside the skeletons are dancing.

Paradise,
the seating of company
    and the defying of gravity,
the teeth recessional again
and the nose in place:
        all burdens are set aside, feet
shoulder and knees.
Here, then
    the products of shipwreck,
a bottle,
a hairpiece and sour lemons,
        dead fish in the water,
a chicken,
and the survivors
    come from the sea resurrected
as calaveras.

[I could put the pot on the table, the dipper,
arrange the silver and napkins
supply the salt cellar.
              Stupidity of lost opportunity,
the *mariachis* are playing again
and I can't be there.
        Stupidity at public gatherings,
lies and deception.
I could shrink down into these bones, under
this flimsy clothing.
        I think I'll do that.
No more stories to tell.
The hair fallen out at the crown.]

. . . this fire, this chicken, this story, these
mariachis and survivors dancing,
      smell of dead fish and whispers
of jetsam from shipwreck in this quiet sea.
This good fellowship
and the presence of women in this telling.
        Pass over the bottle now and the lemon.
Calaca, pinch me a pinch of salt.
We have nowhere to get to, nothing to do.
And this is paradise.

Prayer of Initiation

I pray upon entrance
into the Brotherhood of Endings.
I've given up my feet as offering
to the end of walking around.
    Soon enough, forgetfulness,
first marker of stupor,
confusing machines
and the clicking of various appliances
misunderstood as voices.
    Dear Brotherhood,
that Sisterhood might tend me
even in anger at my early leaving,
even in disgust,
that phrases in our rambling conversations
act as germination of wisdom's ideas
for somebody's children.
    After decline into no stamp collecting
or gardening, into nothing recognizable
as work or even significant
statement to turn heads momentarily,
after lyrics and fingers
losing their way in mud shuffles
among keys and strings, what then
but this Brotherhood, this prayer of endings?
    I went south to Galveston.
I thought upon the shark constantly moving
and the brothers behind curtains in old houses.
I went east to New Bedford
and thought there upon the vegetables
I once tended, a garden gone now
to seed and new growth
of weeds, wild and apprehensive
in their disorderly beginnings.
    The possible became dreaming in waking,

the acutely intimate the distances
at the outward signs.
All the sisters, in triage
have traveled away elsewhere
to tend others. Where now are my brothers?
I cannot see or hear them
and have forgotten
all these beginnings before the end.

Accident of the Axe

As perhaps you have recently noted, given
the cooler, the steel head, and the ankle,
there was considerable pain immediately after

though very little in the way of blood.
I sat down on the stump itself, alone
but for my wife

who was off somewhere picking berries.
Certainly, I was responsible, and there in the ice
in deep throbbing, I thought about this:

no fault of the axe, tree, or the sunlight.
And I thought about walking out
into the sunlight, coming forth

from under the shadows of branches.
In this morning of a new day,
I could walk all the way to Stockholm,

at least to Cairo, Illinois, the nearest big town.
In Cairo was a Swedish woman I was fooling with then
who lived in a white house with four children,

a house my wife had driven by slowly.
I know this because the woman had seen her
and the jig was up, temporarily.

But recently we had started up again,
and I was thinking of the playset in her front yard,
hopping around on the lawn with her children.

Perhaps the look of her was in my eyes,
or it was my own look as I came into her in memory,
melted away with her. I can't be sure,

but I was ready to walk all the way to Cairo.
Then my wife came up to me, right into my face,
then saw the foot in the grass beside me

probably thinking at first it was some animal.
"That's your reward!" she cried out flushed in anger,
then fell down dead at the cooler.

Her berry can had strewn its contents on the ground,
a sort of red coagulant beside the foot.
I felt very much like walking away to get help.

I bought the axe near the Swedish woman's house,
my lame excuse for going over that way.
Perhaps it was barrenness that caused the fatal rage.

Never mind the axe, the shadows, or the sunlight.
Accidents happen, and it's only the insurance policy
I write about. Never mind the Swedish woman either.

This is my claim. All the premiums were paid up.
I'm on crutches and a veteran of foreign wars.
You can send the check ahead to Cairo.

At Some Time

Are the gigolos nervous?
I can't tell.
      That one in tights
and sequins?
           It's swell
that the party went your way
at the end, though clearly every night
was a new beginning.

      Yet I was lonesome, 3 AM
and nothing to do but watch them.
Sure, I could drive you home
at first light.
What right had I to refuse
the dancing?

"You're nothing
      but a strumpet."
"And you, my dear, are nutless."
      Just driving along, typically,
before your blood on the seat.

At some time or other,
      we were, I guess, "happy
to see you. Did you sleep well?"
      Or do I imagine that you spoke
gently over breakfast.
Then somebody just appeared,
that one in sequins.

Machinery of forensics,
      as on television, your car
completely dismantled,
      for blood is telltale as testament

to all-seeing detectives,
just gigolos like all the others.
You deserved it, luckily
the axe was handy.

[The body's tenderness: I'd overdriven
    those barricades,
lucky in love, then attention
at the right time.
        Axe into flesh?
The bright warning signs were yellow.
    A complete awareness of fragility
since then.
It could have been otherwise.]

Stunned, ever since then, by lack of wisdom.
The obvious escaped them.

[Obeisant to the trees
    that give us paper, housing
and shade,
the handle is wooden.
Though the blade bite deep,
    there's no bleeding
but for sap.
    The scalpel, something
else entirely, is made for flesh.
But I was put to sleeping then
and did not cry out.]

Running ever since then with gigolos,
wearing sequins
    cut away in fabric taken
from your dresses. Our eyes are upon

money, sister,
what's provided by cruel and lonely women.
          You were the one exception
at some time or another, over breakfast:
have a nice day. The way
you spoke when you weren't screaming.

[Some other accidents: pricking a finger,
    just imagine the whole hand
lopped off. Won't muscles contract,
        squeezing the arteries against
too much bleeding?
    The delicate white neck, shaving,
swell of the barked knuckle,
her fragile temple, the car seat.]

Over this time I am losing energy.
    I get sick on the off nights,
not from guilt,
        but increasing remembrances
of good times, which is loss.
Do you remember, of course you can't now,
times at the beach
    when we were younger, traveling
down Mexico way for enchiladas,
        sum sum Summertime
and those other foolish songs
from our generation?
    Look at that one, she's ready,
but I have no heart for it.
        "What kind of day did you have?"
over dinner.

[Accident of the head turning too suddenly,
something in the neck.]

That's what I said, over dinner,
and later,
 at times during the entire evening,
"What kind of day did you have?"
  "Would you like a cocktail?"
Then sleeping,
just the two of us
in sweet oblivion, together.

[Stronger than a vicious tide, able to leap
to the room's center, then call out
over the bed to the sleeping lovers:
 This Ends in Tragedy.
Yet who is that,
but indulged imagination?
  All the wounds would be real,
sharp, chopping cuts on the palms, defensive,
visible brain matter,
 like wet gobs ripped away
from a natural sponge, in her temple.]

Please indulge me. Please try to understand.
 It was the dancing, my desire
for gigolos
until I was one of them
 and with them, a breath of clean air.
It wasn't difficult to kill her,
 the axe was there, but it was
this other thing, I say love
and its attendant madness that drove me.
Beyond reason?

Can this forgive me?
     I sleep alone these days,
stay to the side when among gigolos.
I always try to dance
        with the best dancer.
She reminds me of you.

[It seems so long that I have been waiting
     for the knife, the gun, the sledge hammer
and the axe. I even anticipate the needle, my red
blood rising in the tube.
         I wait, of course, with trepidation
for the undesired.
Would a stroke be the same, a heart attack:
just a brief pain, and then nothing?
     No wonder this fascination with the implement,
strategies for putting it off.]

No statute of limitations, but time goes by.
The memory goes by, and the vessel
holding the memory, that too goes by.

[Remember, when we were children,
     I stepped on glass in the river,
or the time
I fell, and have since
named it The Broken Clavicle?
     Certainly there is pain's echo
in new pain: this is like
that time, though of this time only.
     The memory goes by, but the vessel
holding the memory
carries the evidence of it, these scars
that can ache at times.

    I call them The Statutes, meaning
position or status,
  a ruler to measure the down slope,
or possibly, when half-dreaming,
it's the canvas in which I am written.]

Of brotherhood, when they are lovers,
  and of cruel, beautiful women:
gigolos
are made for dancing, escorting,
consorting against husbands who have
  worn out their welcome.
Cavorting?
I've a vague memory of a river,
  wasn't it glass,
and your pretty foot cut in the wading?
Didn't we do something intimate after?
  I thought of it briefly
when I twisted my ankle
dancing.
  But time moves on
and I grow too old for romancing.
I've packed my bag. Farewell to women
and gigolos,
even the one in sequins,
  who started all this. Hey, Jose,
Bye Bye.

Theatrical Story

Rivers can rise romantically above their banks
at flood tide, in movies; there may be women
in shifts in good shape clinging to chimneys.
They are not yet my desire.

Just as I was about to enter.
As she was leaving.
After the party but before sleeping.
Down by the riverside in moonlight.

The story grows more complex over the years,
ho hum, no others care for this drama.
I was running ahead to save her,
possibly a stitch in time. Nobody cares.

Light as a single tortilla, the damaged dancer,
south of the border, to have chased her
in the music of mariachis, tripping
under bougainvillea, down Mexico way.

And nobody cares for the politician,
his mother and father, those who were saintly
and taught him the right road: applause
from the audience, tentative. Empty orchestra.

I keep using that term. Is it empty
of singers, conductor, even the instruments?
Nobody cares for the passing years, but
for the movies, those entertainments.

Just as I was about to enter, in Mexico,
she was leaving on her crutches.
After the party but before sleeping together,
tentatively, down by the riverside in moonlight.

Standard-16, I Remember You

     Like the memory of that moody jazz
leaking out under tent flaps
        at a California pleasure fair
or pages scattered from a long forgotten book,
word fertilizer
helping flowers seed,
blossom and become vegetables for bees,
how often have I cast
     these things aside, only
to retrieve them again, transformed,
soiled and degraded?

That summer . . .
     That fall before winter avocados
fell from their brittle stems,
        ignorant of them
in our own green flush,
     what ancillary music
did we brighten our smoggy days with
against various futures and ambitions?

The thrill of it all,
        light as a feather fallen
from some passing jay,
minus that awakening call.
We were the rage
of our sixties circle, which included
only us.

I can't remember you too well,
     but like an old shoe
found deep in the dark closet,
        you left that clothing in haste,
and I was glad for it,

         your limping at Lillian Way,
half shod in the stench of eucalyptus
and grinning sheepishly.
         How romantic, these remainders:
old devil unmentionables
and deflated beach ball for devil sun.

Nothing is like anything else.
The rain falls in fog all afternoon,
    then stutters along into early evening,
when the breeze dies down
for moratorium, and the pine candles
are stiff sentinels.
         Then we have that stillness,
ladies and gentlemen, in which dead time
is for memory's reconstructions,
if only from a few fleeting details.

    It's much like the rain itself,
a little depressing,
but it helps flowers grow, even though
nothing is like anything else.

You're often the one
downstage among so many others,
    mother's wishes for a sisterhood
of like minded souls,
         a host of dead friends
and mild mannered enemies waiting
in the shadowy wings,
for a little while (a moment ago?),
    from a distance,
inaccessible
and fortified by a brew of Sangria
fashioned from local fruits.

Just lying around, just
putting our feet up on the coffee table,
 just heading out on the Triumph
for the vineyards, carefully
my dears, for I'm alone now in memory
and not saddle sore. What's more,
 there seems a dozen of you there
behind me on the buddy-seat.

From time to time
 I danced in the foyer,
sad to remember.
 I cannot speak of adult comfort,
whatever that is,
just being in one place at a time.

Like nothing else after stormy weather,
young grapes on the vine,
 the beginning of a wine fashion
in the Napa Valley;
we might have fallen
 down in the vineyard itself
to watch them grow,
though Gallo in a jug those days for us,
 the start of darker days
of no common sense at all:
 married in the name only
of love and not money
or any comparable maturity,
light as a fallen feather, glandular.

A strumpet?
Chet Baker's voice and trumpet? Those angles
of repose along the river bed

            in the town of El Monte
when I was much younger,
before that wisdom I still don't have.
      Embraceable you or any other
was quite enough.

Mother?,
no psychology of that kind,
      yet family's gradual unhingement.
I had collies to tend to
        and a victim of surgery,
legs splayed beside her crutches.
We talked and ate dog food in the kitchen
behind mood music
and the painful burning
      in such tortured love,
though it was not only that.

I could take a rhythm break
      in the wistfulness
of Brubeck and Desmond,
just listen
as if it were my pulse beating.
I won't do that.

The moon's bright and hard now,
full and dimensional,
      in the night's sky after rain.
There is no music in this reality after all,
just smokey scents from chimneys,
counterpoint to a dog's barking.

I think you might be happier,
less sleepy,

      if I told a story,
whether true or constructed
from degraded details:
hearts and flowers on a prom dress,
that kind of thing, Marie
      in 1953, before cappuccino,
sushi, and those other
           sophisticated trappings,
moon over the water and its river
upon the magic lake.
      It couldn't ever be casual,
a catalogue of names
followed us into our tents.
Then the deer came.
Or was it coyote, ferocious javelinas,
somebody's horse
      loose in the desert mountains,
a skunk caught in the trap we'd laid,
close to fatherless, Paul and I?

I saw him once later,
      married and gotten religion,
but then it was my dream, also a howling.
He crept into the tent
      quietly to soothe me,
himself too, since I was huffing
      and there might have been something
out there.
It was a dream of death wished for,
that I had brought ending
      to our absent fathers,
yet seemed more than a dream.

But Marie!
Hidden as the towhee sings tentatively
    and does not reveal herself
in the morning, light as the leaves
and brown tipped also
    in fall foliage,
what fragments of song can I call up
to soothe you, those degraded past tunes
of our ridiculous venture:
Heart of my heart, I had the craziest dream,
Moon River?

It seems even sinister
    now that the moon's glow
sings in the pines' candles, turning trees
to a semblance of women
    in spiky dresses or shrouds
set piecemeal
in the clear night beyond my window,
    just watching, or accusing me.
The song
might then be a dirge, though the tune
was once popular.

One more time: fish gotta swim,
birds fly,
    the bees get hooked
on pollen, myopically,
all the fragments seem in order,
like these pine trees
or that scent of eucalyptus,
    rancid still in virginity,
before it becomes cleansing
designer soap.

      I remember you
beyond justice or understanding,
as if we were reconstructed
to begin yet again,
a little bit of that longing,
          faint scent of romance,
the potion clarified now
in the music I thought then
      would focus and simplify
the shadow of your smile
and, in reality, the way I felt.

Six Short Poems

1. Windsock

Sing windsock fall stars
    fret vacant eyes
in cloudy wing drifts
turning back to summer and you
new moon
level at horizon. Soon
    winter icing the shield
grease thickening our kind
shivering in cockpit's vacancy
of spring
which will never come
    to this sky's quarter
but will creep in
uncelebrated
    until we think ahead
to summer.

2. Passenger

Little unknown passenger once slung
diabetic candy on the shoulder
for balance
awhile to hold down chicory
    moving coffee mist
here in the mountains' freedom
from sickness
    of hanging bottles bandages
carabiner crutches a cane
that's sugar
parceled out in pyramids
    among trees under the sun

    darkening the moon
glow in four hands joined
to form a stretcher
across the fire.

3. In Thrall

Tangible in regard to money's
    tuneful reversals new hat
worn down carefully
the style
of spending and getting
    brassy trombones rubber
planters a ring
for your delicate third finger
    last month's credit card bills
even the earth
held thrall to shopping
    a showplace
yet moving
beyond the static state
    of a breviary taken in hand
whose canonical hours
roll by over litter not rotting
but for caviar
forgotten in the fridge.

4. Dancing Shoes

Evermore in past hours
    on feet in dancer's shoes
buckled and high bows

          lyrical as that melody
played too fast
for this developing limp
     brought on by winter rain
soaking laces and various
metatarsus.
A story of worry fleshed out now
in time after times
     on the beach in the mountains
any court or dance
floor superior at such things
     though not others.
Animal magnetism the foxtrot lifting
its weary head
     to somebody else's feet
in the dancer's shoes
     goes by carefully noted
on the way of the world.

5. Fishing

Glandular regard
     of the stumblebums whose tents
along the river lift
in wind to settle once again
     after a good dinner
of crappie
and bluegill lunging at the bait cast
through great attention
free of reeds. Now soon after the wives
have gone down
     for civilized dancing
where the town's lights blink

in branches
of glorious promise
   urged on by camping
fishing manly eyes
on stars in the river
free now
and can talk like children.

6. Young Girl

It's late in the house and the girl
at summer's end in fire
  of fake hearth-logs purchased
from a boy stirring
something new yet remembered
in the tribe's life
of flesh repetitiously cooked up
   in centuries of the living
room where she now sits
  awkwardly cannot find
her spot.
Be still my foolish heart.

Border Towns

Towns along the border
    seem to wake up when I enter them,
fresh squeezed
and hotcakes, or griddle
depending on which side you're on.
The thought of crossing over
    has me longing for return
almost immediately. Most often
there are fences, but not always
in mountains:
natural boundaries, fjords and gorges,
and sometimes there are troops
    at the demarkation
in defense or aggression,
gunboats even in narrow rivers.

I have not taken sufficient time
to mourn them,
    sent on their journeys
without backpacks or other accoutrements,
though I did creep up in the night
for a good look
before deciding on retreat.
    Borders are not benign mappings,
towns often seething like countries
before war.
I wished only to enter and then be gone,
but they had left things behind,
and I was stuck with them.

There,
at the gate marking the entrance
or the exclusion, there,
    given the sight lines,

crossing seems less than treacherous,
but coming back?:
that town
on the hill in the far distance,
  its warren of confusing streets.
I thought I had the answers
to all things measured, before departing.

Summer comes, then fall, then winter
  snow drifts against the barricades, [and] here
the ones who cover their ears up in the slightest breeze.
Should spring ever come again to this border town
[given the sight lines]
and those living without guile sufficient for dishonesty.
  To the one whose undergarments are soiled by sweat
and clots of blood in childbirth anciently
[before deciding], and to the derelict in the dead of winter,
her filthy hair, the ones [on retreat]
without energy for young children, their filthy hair.
  Should spring ever come forth again [in mountains]
to these tree skeletons and the girls who wish to dance,
   the square dance, the tango, the ones who dress
for winter even in the early fall.
[Depending on which side you're on], depending on the tune
of fire trucks and the strapping on of explosives, then
to the memory of burning leaves and the houses
ablaze in the burning, tree skeletons [without] and children
playing in the leaves [before war].
  [Not] unto the cold hammer, to the flesh under the hammer
[to mourn them], should spring ever come,
  but to the last effort, the final ditch, and the one
who stands romantic at the bedside in memory of seamen
and the pines spilling their hazy pollen [always]
in menses beyond the window and the soiled underwear.

[I have not taken sufficient time]
for the [borders are not] towns and the ones [sent on their
 journeys] stand guard at the gates, [its towns]
[in defence or aggression], nor for the dark soil
under the snow, the stink of compost, weather palaver,
and overheated radiators.
 The people stand in the town square, cold down even
to their private parts. [Most often] the officials
positioned [on the hill in the far distance]
 come to believe [almost immediately]
that the [crossing seems less than treacherous]. The fathers
who have no taste for the winter mothers and drink hot milk
with nutmeg as if they were children, bang each other
 on the shoulders and don't shave [for a good look].
And the fires are now burning
 in the [warren of confusing streets],
in the red hair of the ones under abuse and the sleeves
of the women dancing, on tables, in bones and long dresses,
who are the calaveras
who dance away death [at the gate marking the entrance
or the exclusion].
Never will spring come to [them], [hotcakes or griddle],
to the [towns]
 shivering in [benign mappings] of band formations,
ridiculous costumes and [other accoutrements], icy tuba
bells, [stuck with] epaulets, after marching to melodies
of mounted police music [before departing].
Fires [seem to wake up], as if in celebration of spring coming
[along the border], electric where [there are fences].
 Fires burn in the deep [gorges], on rafts upon [fjords],
as if the sun [had left] light behind [fresh squeezed]
in the night sky, left to [creep up in the night]
insanely, as converse [to all things measured] carefully
 [I thought I had the answers]

before attendant forgetting, to [that] talk as tumultuous
        background, the noise [but] even of fruit flies
constant under that babble, orange stands [and] brass bands
[there] at the [town] center,
[but] ice under the hill, in the cracked cup,
in arthritic fingers and radiators, in trumpet valves,
shoelaces, all [things behind] in forgotten shadow
[when I enter them].
    [I wished only to enter and then be gone].
[But they], the fires, are burning along the fences
        having found a delineation at the scorched skin,
[and sometimes there are] pyres [seething
like countries] rising up against borders [there]
as if a dry flint struck for sudden ignition.
    All the towers are burning, the bridges,
[gunboats even in the narrow rivers] have been set aflame.
The houses and [backpacks] are burning, the churches,
    even the coffee shop I entered, [and I was]
in arrogance, at first light.
The snow is melting in the heat of burning
        at the barricade fences, [often] promising:
Perhaps it's spring!
[Or] all the borders are opening,
    but it's too late.
Even though people are running [coming back] swiftly,
their bodies burning
        as they pass others, also torches,
approaching the [natural boundaries],
    [troops at the demarcation],
[the thought of] their town entered [crossing over]
[has me] returning with them [though I did]
upon leaving, from the other side.

Reversal of Fortunes

Beyond the orchestrated placement of the child's hands,
    fingers laced among seemingly strewn flowers,
in one of a number of cities
       where multitudes are allowed still to blossom,
men out of uniform at the periphery
photograph the bearers,
    whose burden seems light as a feather
and might actually rise up,
as borne on the Prophet's robes.

It's Sunday; it might be any day
in the recording,
everything soon to be solved,
and above the newspaper,
    hard rain holds acid in the early light
streaking my windows and disordered thoughts;
puddles rise into rivers
       along the gravel walkways,
stones vibrant and variously
multitudinous
as the world's children, as if bathed in oil.

    [Who would treat my body
to such soothing pleasure,
       sisters, mother, my grandmother?
Better to have felt my limbs in their hands
at some earlier time.]

    The grandmother once played by his gramophone,
a reversal of fortune, in a photograph
of a life spent wholesomely in a quiet town.

Bearers, can you spare a dime, for travel,
for the reversal of fortune of a child whose body
is quiet-town-wholesome, for a spent life?

[In a tape recording played by my grandmother],
on a gramophone, sisterhood to a spent life.
Is a dime given for quiet travel, wholesomely?

[I have nowhere to go, my grandmother's quiet town?]
The river reverses the fortunes of fishermen.
The streets become littered with bodies and gramophones.

The repetitious recording of the river is vicious
travel reversal of fortunes for spent children
who play gramophones along parkways and quiet streets.

    [A dead town, a town for mothers] to spend life's dime.
Those who are wholesome are heard only on gramophones
or on tape recorders, spared for quiet travel reversals.

[If they had just oiled my ruined body, if they had just
laced long fingers between my piggy toes.]

The casual machine of childhood, a dime spun quietly
for travel, vicious restrictions, a tape's reversal,
so that one listens to fortunes spilling from grandmothers.

Or from rivers of gramophones, wholesome fishermen who are
tape recorders, unfortunate children along ruined parkways.
Each reversal turns littered streets to a spent quiet-town.

    A dead town, a town of reversals and restrictions,
of life spent on rivers littered with spent fishermen,
broken recorders. [I have nowhere to play, for fortune.]

The body is lifted now casually into the sun;
    the grandmothers beat at their clothing.
Perhaps the flowers are falling
into the hair of the sisters,

          the mothers who stumble
into the cameras' perspectives.
But the bearers have been recorded,
these spent fishermen in this quiet town
        [a dead town] of reversals and restrictions.
I am fortunate in this stormy day,
these river pathways.

[If only it would rain
        to silence my grandmother and her gramophone,
to wash away this spent litter.
        If only they could spin
a dime for travel.]

My grandmother tells a story of reversal in a dead town,
a tape recording of the police chief, now a mortician,
his spent marriage, his son, his wife's gramophone.

[I fly for refuge unto the Lord of the daybreak],
to the dead-town marriage motel's violent restrictions
beside rivers littered with fortunes of dead children.

Reversal of a casual machine, the gramophone, multitudes
of pills to commemorate their union. [That He may deliver me
from the mischief of those things which He hath created.]

And rushes with his son on the spent dime, wholesomely
in the quiet town, passing rivers littered with fishermen,
tape recordings, photographs, everything soon to be solved.

No pills, but a barrel at her temple as the door opens again
and again, vicious repetition. [And let not compassion
toward them prevent you from executing the judgement.]

Now the litter is lowered down into the quiet town,
      the body wrapped up in the flowers,
child-size in the winding sheets.
         Yet the vicious recording continues
in photographs, gramophones of the grandmothers,
      tape recordings of the sisters.
A dead town of the mothers,
everything soon to be solved
         not by fishermen, seemingly strew flowers
on the unfortunate banks of reversed rivers,
not by the spinning of dimes spared
for quiet travel arrival
      into His taped presence
[who hath created man of congealed blood]
repetitiously recorded
in a litter of gramophones along spent parkways.

      A quiet town of police chiefs and morticians,
rivers along gravel walkways, vibrant and variously
multitudinous as the world's children bathed in oil.

      A dead town, a town of reversals and restrictions,
of violent fortunes in gramophones and honeymoon litter,
so that a wife can spin dimes for a smoking barrel.

The repetitious recording of the reversed river is vicious
highway of the bearers lifting burdens on the Prophet's robes.
Those who are wholesome are heard only on gramophones.

The casual machine of childhood travel, flying for refuge,
passing by parkways and rivers littered with spent fortunes.
The strewn fishermen, who might be fathers, are restricted.

Out of uniform at the periphery, photographs, on a dime spent
for litter of dead children, broken gramophones and mothers.
Sudden reversal of the casual machine, doth not prevent them.

[He will assist you against your enemies
        and will set your feet fast, but not for travel,
that reversal of a fortune in my piggy toes.
If they had just
        laced long fingers between them,
had oiled my body,
even with slick sludge
        in rivers littered from passage of His
amphibians through them,
who is provided with everything
and suffers not the work of any worker.]

The rain releases its fortunes into the dead town.
Petals fall like bright dimes into the sisters' hair.
The river reverses again and is cleansed of litter.

His grandmother's gramophone and tape recorder are spun
on a dime quietly, for travel, for maps of the town
no longer viciously restricted to men out of uniform.

No longer restricted to police chiefs and morticians,
their sons, and their wives reversing fortunes of pills
for smoking barrels at the doorways of marriage motels.

The casual machine of childhood, wholesome fishermen
beyond the barricades, everything soon to be solved.
The rain reverses the fortunes of the dead town's creation.

        A quiet town, rain water, burdens light as a feather.
In your last dream, He will lift you on the Prophet's robes
and will admit you into gardens, through which rivers flow.

That's a Thought

Maybe I should drop you off,
park the car and walk back.
      Last time, I lost out.
If you will just
stay put, I can manage,
knowing which way to head.

I should drop you out, stay put,
and just manage last time.
      Knowing which way to head off,
I lost the car.
Maybe, if you will park, I can
walk back.

Park the car. I should stay put,
knowing I lost which way to head
      last time, walk back out,
just drop you off.
And maybe, if I can manage,
you will.

If you will just stay put,
knowing which way to head.
[too soon we are coming to grief]
      That's a thought
I can manage last time.
Maybe I should walk back,
[in a dark hysterical day]
drop you off and park the car.

Last time, knowing I should park,
[counting the hours waiting]
maybe drop you,
      if you will just stay put.

That's a thought.
[even when it was blood raining]
I could look around, walk back,
and manage which way to head.

[perhaps the city will soon be burning]
Surely, you'll be waiting.
Maybe I should drop you off and stay put.
    I could look around.
[all the leaders are without ethics]
That's a thought.
If you will just manage,
knowing which way to head back.

If you will stay put and manage, knowing
which way to head, I could look around.
    That's a thought,
[shamed by a crude arrogance]
stunned into somnolence.
Surely, you'll be waiting.
[assassination a commonplace]
Maybe I should drop back.

I could look around and maybe manage,
stunned into somnolence.
    Who's directing this traffic?
[hath not a penchant for understanding]
That's a thought I should drop, stay put.
Surely, you'll be waiting,
[the hammer of the iron will]
knowing which way to head.

Who's directing this traffic?
[birth unto ignorance unto death]

knowing which way to head,
    the outward sign,
stunned into somnolence: that's a thought.
[little time left for a quickening]
I could look around, maybe stay put
and manage. Surely, you'll be waiting.

Palaver of the cruel occupations, stunned
[the blind leading the blind]
into somnolence, the outward sign.
    Who's directing this traffic?
That's a thought. I could look around,
[unto this certain evil]
Surely, you'll be waiting, knowing
which way to head.

That's a thought, I could look around.
Surely, you'll be waiting,
    stunned into somnolence.
Who's directing this traffic?
The outward sign. Palaver of the cruel
occupations. Perhaps the city is burning.

Palaver stunned into the outward sign,
the cruel city is burning,
    I could look around this,
the thought surely of directing a somnolence.
Who's waiting? Perhaps you'll be.
Occupations, that's traffic.

Perhaps you'll be around. I could look.
The outward traffic is burning.
    That's a thought waiting somnolence
of the city sign,

surely stunned into the occupations.
Who's directing this cruel palaver?

Too soon we are coming to grief
in a dark hysterical day,
          counting the hours waiting
even when it was blood raining.
     Perhaps the city will soon be burning.
All the leaders are without ethics,
shamed by a crude arrogance.

Assassination a commonplace,
hath not a penchant for understanding
         the hammer of the iron will.
Birth unto ignorance unto death,
    little time left for a quickening,
the blind leading the blind
unto this certain evil.

Gallery

A child standing before a blackboard.
        A ragamuffin standing before a stone wall.
Something is given: a hand, a mask, a piece of chalk.
There, in the left side of the chest.

Having deciding on a honeymoon trip fashioned
        for other parties, flowers in her hair.
Figures only from maps upon arrival.
To the right side facing a child, underhanded.

Something is cast aside: a ring, a knife, a garter.
        Ghost of dalmatian's head above the cowcatcher.
Having expected another vehicle entirely.
Fire in awakening on the station platform.

Only to find it is time now for sleeping.
        A child high in the air over water.
As much as they have carved out and anticipated.
Having discovered little in this pipe dream.

Something discovered in the dark zone.
        Under the sternum: a tin can, strapping, a bomb.
A child's arm high in the air over water.
Electricity's burst at the architect's window.

Limping down a country path at the dead end of summer.
Frail asters, a ragamuffin, pathetic rear guard.
        The bride stands flushed at the gate.
Something on the ground: a ring, a skeleton traveler.

A party fashioned only for strangers.
        The groom stands at the gate in a fur hat.
Ice-crusted pines through a foggy window.
The other: gone south into sinister places.

Against onslaught of that winter's coming
    in a frosty train down from a distance.
Pipes and hot tea, something burning.
A child dancing in electrified tethers.

Of a country garden: cans, bolts and wires.
    Something among the living at the bride's feet.
Tea, in degrees dipping through the narrow windshield.
[Did I mistake this for a real romance?]

In the aftermath of the war the war continues.
    A child selling the news before a barricade.
[someone like you]
After the fallen bride: on the ground, a ring.

Festival Dancers dead in their tracks at the ceremony.
    The architect moves in sludge to the window's map.
There, in the left side of the chest.
[I wish I knew]: something on the ground, frail asters.

The wish set forth on a train into the future.
    Figures only from maps upon arrival.
[if you don't care]
Skeletons dance in the Festival Dancers' outfits.

Having expected another vehicle entirely.
[But you can only answer me]: a thing, a piece of metal.
    This, picture of the ground on which . . .
Fire of the groom dancing in flames at the ceremony.

After the declarations [I wish I knew], marriage or war.
    The child stands before walls, vehicles, borders.
He carries the bride into the honeymoon chamber.
Having discovered little in this pipe dream.

Returning then into shelter after the blood-rain.
    The groom slakes passion in drink from a decanter.
Something discovered in the dark zone.
[What should I do?]: this ground, asters, oil.

[Don't lead me on if I'm a fool to say so.]
    The bride stands flushed at the gate.
On the ground. Always on the ground. Under the ground.
The river bears up the dead, still in their costumes.

A party fashioned only for strangers.
    A child standing at judgment before a stone wall.
[Should I keep dreaming on or just forget you?]
At the southern end of the city, flames.

The bride washing herself seen through a foggy window.
    A child dancing in electrified tethers.
The coach comes down, bearing the skeleton figures.
On the ground, something: [I wish I knew.]

The station, ruined in fire in the architect's window.
    Something among the living at the bride's feet.
[Why let me hope and pray so?]: a ragamuffin, a child.
It stands, falling over in the river, its arm in the air.

[You'd place no one could love one above me.]
    In the aftermath of the war the war continues.
The bride is pictured standing against a blackboard.
A ruined map, the ground sucking up all evidence.

The earth is soddened as the mind is with memory.
    The train bears the calaveras in the dancers' costumes.
Having placed the child pressing against a post.
All the barriers. The ground breaking. [I wish I knew.]

In the dark cistern, in the powder puff, delight or death.
    To have ironed out all problems and costumes.
Of the river. In the river. Fallen over.
After we were about to begin again in travel.

The bride and groom. Festival Dancers. The architect.
    Having planned a trip into the south knowing no risk.
Asters strewn on the ground before the garden gate.
Something: a wet hankie, a flag rising as a child's arm.

In time after time is spent the coin and the oil.
    A ragamuffin hangs only as a doll for the news.
The bride is pictured standing beside the groom.
The skeletons dance away flesh at the festival.

Dolls

Little maiden cares so little
for love that when
      her doll breaks open
it's for lost power of manipulation
that she weeps
as much as nursing game.

What innocence has she learned
to set aside
in this cruel world
      for maidens and an evil one
of doll-maker fabricators
who are politicians
forcing through budgets
for weapons?

And war doth not temper them. I saw
the doll face of a child
where she had fallen,
      not as beautiful as the living,
piggy toes pointing
at the smoky sky.

Just as they have come to regard each other
wearily, these lessons are handed down
even to maidens.

And these other dark dolls,
whose toys are cans,
      electrical wires, bolts,
might they let them alone in their playing,
or will they too break open?

Prayer to the Most Powerful Hand

I place my Christian soul before thee
fundamentally, to rid myself of it,
    this despair and anguish,
light the candle
beseechingly against
ruined feet, rescue, devotion,
this destiny of suffering
    that is not mine or theirs,
those "sacred" and profane hearts.

A hand up and a handling
of wonders, loving kindness. But your hand
    becomes a fist, then a hammer,
a sledge in the shape of a book, your
palm on the cover, stigmata,
drives down the homeless, even more
those who are hungry,
for what: faith, belief, surcease
of sorrow? But for food, shelter, shoes,
electricity, water, not
for loving kindness. Justice of Democracy?
What is that here,
    but to be pounded more firmly
under power of hysterical arrogance.

Hand,
come down upon the self-righteous,
    down as a hammer in retribution
upon the "sorrowful hearts"
in their impossible ignorance
and the acid of their ministrations.
    But you will not come down.
Let us pray upon forgiveness,
for strength and wisdom,

for pardon from a destiny of suffering
brought by these limp and fattened wizards
in hiding behind your palm.

    Let us pray in the name of
the most powerful hand
and the fundamental testament.
Then let us close the book that is a hammer
and walk out of the churches forever,
though we be initially blinded
in eternal sunlight and drink sparingly
from the clear pool of forgetfulness
as you wave us away.

        — from the inscription on a holy candle

A Cole Porter Medley

1. I Concentrate On You

Gray skies and winter winds,
so people declare surrender once again
        [an ev'ry time, we say]
on the tender decline,
and blues become the so-so concentrate
too strong to brew: [of] you
and men, [but] on the intertwine.
        Our trouble begins in your eyes dream,
[goodbye] never to prove sweet fortune wise.
Whenever true,
whenever to me wrong, [there's time,
we know] comes through you even on [a] song.
        [Be] your smile, first kiss to me;
you're my only concentrate.
Look, my arms. I can be wise to you
when men say, nay –
        that love's young.
I become light when at that concentrate,
whenever I concentrate
on you.

2. Don't Fence Me In

Oh send me to the ridge
        where cottonwood trees ride [on] the moon.
Let me gaze at the wide land, murmur, and wander
off to forever underneath the mountains.
        I can't [concentrate and] fence the stand
of open country,
[nay] western skies above.
Can't [I] rise to straddle the fences in me?
[When you] listen, look at [me]

the hobbles. Let me in.
Don't give me
    the evening breeze on lots of starry skies.
I want my cayuse, my old saddle, over yonder,
under the land that I don't love.
    Let me be myself, lose my senses [and you].
Don't fence till I see
    [when] the West commences.
Please, don't ride thru me.
Just turn me loose.

3. Ev'ry Time We Say Goodbye

Strange, the gods, little lark
    somewhere in the air above me,
you're near [me] to [let me]
begin [in] spring
    ev'ry time I die
from the change to minor.
[I ask you] must we say goodbye?
[But] I wonder a little why
    I allow you to [fence me in], go
sing finer,
[till I] say major about it
[in] no love song.
How they think of me when, so little,
there's such a goodbye [fence]
about it.
    Who can hear ev'ry why?
Ev'ry single time
we say goodbye.

Note: Every word of each refrain (and only these) is used in the poems. Residual words from 1 enter 2 in brackets, and so on in a circle.

Too Late Now

Carefully, but any time [too late]
      the flesh in carelessness
[now to forget]
places itself, distracting [your smile]
        upon the hearth
or in memory [the way] of pain
[one word] calls out,
the hour then rolls around [makes]
      in which the marker [my heart]
of lost capability can shine
and [rejoice] then, only to close
        [close] down [darling, no]
fragments [danced awhile],
    I am urged on to the clock,
though [imagine myself]
        release temporary suffering
under this burden of chopped ice
[anymore].

Forgetfulness, [the way we cling]
after the bad [done] deed,
    after [tender] discovery,
what is this but loss and perversity
of freedom, my hand not on the
        hearth then, but stung
in abuse of another [stays]?
To return [and be the same
      as I was before] and go before judges,
but [someone new] yet to remember
the body, the sting, slamming
[the door].

Yet for reward, passionate as the clock,
tumblers dropping in the lock,

[to forget and go on] for this
[I relive] in remembrance of [your voice]
your shocked face, I
turn not [away from you]
to the crimes. Whatever the hammer,
      the red hearth [my heart], that soothing
of chopped ice in sink
or bucket, [all the things] it's no good
to count days and hours,
      to measure against
some chart of the possible
[when we're apart]
and not very likely [together].
It lives [on in] only in the textures,
[too late now] to confuse [fun]
with some distant idea
      of seriousness, [to forget]
which is life's illusion [too late]
arrived at [now] in anger,
          [now] in laughter, [to] go
and then [to] return, refreshed
saying [how could I ever] I'm sorry [now],
though it was [too late]
and well after.

Sustenance,
[when we've] returned for cruelty,
      [all the] hard times awaiting us
[together] yet amount to nothing
in light of this.
Mark it down on the chart, let the
tumblers fall.
      After coming a good long way,
[we've] let the mix of ice and hearth

continue. The clock strikes [no]
      the hours and days,
imagines a time when it will all
be over. [I can't] It's too late now
[It's too late now].

My Little Plane

1

Perhaps the air will let
my little plane down
to sink into that imprint
on the land in the lens's watermark
finally upon paper
      which is a map impossible
of that size for understanding like
me and my mom like it was awesome
in a language inadequate
          unto the darklight
and the warning light at the door
developing what can never be approached
in the shadow
under the shadow.

2

I saw a woman hidden in a lava
declivity
      my little plane's shadow
at the periphery near a bowl
of water stagnant in blue absence
        of past activity or perhaps
it was a man impossible to be certain
in a language inadequate
from this altitude
      was missing or lost love
that unspecified yearning
developing what can never be approached
as I was working my way
back to you.

3.

Adventure of the shadow of my little plane
fixed on film and in the memory
    of a hovering over sea
though it was land looking like waves
from this altitude
and higher still were daystars
also invisible in
        that unspecified yearning
for a past deeper in some other anatomy
that I might be touching
though only through shadows
of myself behind uncertain lenses
    in this constant droning
of the engine like the world's turnings.

4.

So then was traveling through smoke
above such archeology
    which is a plundering
like me and my mom
    like it was awesome figures
from a past inadequate
in this constant droning
of a language
that I might be touching
you on the earth bound up
in complexity ancient as memory
    of a time fashioned from childhood
when we stepped fresh from the cockpit
at least it seemed that way.

5.

Ice threatens before fire
 under the warming
of my little plane's shadow
and hearth light aglow there beckoning
you on the earth bound up
 in such glacial imagination
could freeze into a fixture
to then percolate
in this heated nostalgia
at least it seemed that way
high up as I was
thinking to fall
 down into animal memory
inhuman and finally alone.

6.

Two thousand over big island skylight
thinking to fall
 as much wish as a dream
of my little plane casket descending
into the orange eye
 to then percolate
in the blue field
which is night's hoard and endless
like it was awesome like
 a gestural language without
me and my mom like turning
into a past absent
of all memory sufficient
unto nostalgia.

7.

Like it was awesome like
a valley smoking its own anatomy
    under which another surface
of a kind of skin
peeled back and revealing
    yet another no longer
a mystery but a shadow
under a shadow
of all memory sufficient
    unto the task forgotten
as I was drifting in the realization
that the lens too is a false framing
the world's turnings myopic
in the watermark stain of my little plane.

8.

Like me and my mom like were walking
through a desert and came into
    a mystery but a shadow
to cool us as we looked up finding
the little plane casting a watermark
down upon us who were trying
    hard to give vent to our
broken relationship in this wilderness
unto the task forgotten
    as I imagined myself in the plane
my shadow a stain to provide like an awning
to give her some comfort
correct for a son or a daughter yet I
in another story entirely.

9.

We were looking out to a far horizon
like me and my mom were like inside
  in another story entirely
a Rothko painting of the earth's hues
in changing greens and the sky's blues
over Brittany coming
    down upon us who were trying
to right our relationship in the cockpit
of my little plane
which of itself was fragility drifting
  almost invisible in a soup
like Rothko's paint like me and my mom
the whole sky was an awesome home
and we were at comfort in it.

10.

Under the shadow of lava in the lens
perhaps a father awaits me as a lover
almost invisible in a soup
  crowded with images existent only
in this sentimental and foolish eye
but to each his own
    and the earth is beautiful if violent
and can be like me and my mom
like I can be a baby girl or boy again
and wouldn't that be awesome
  but like very painful
and I brought my eye back to the cockpit
only to find I was there and here
which of itself was fragility drifting.

11.

Imagine the water a shadow figure
in this sentimental and foolish eye
      the land a face seen from a satellite
youth the green beyond the ancient cuts
like plastic surgery
      to bring youth back
and wouldn't that be awesome
though having suffered for the gain
supposing violence
      of time could be forestalled
before the figure under the shadow
becomes finally fixed
and the sea no more than a blue wash
spied in the lens.

12.

The human past is dead
      though this earth rise up violent
and beautiful red in the lens
to bring youth back
      like me and my mom
before the figure under the shadow
is revealed
      as a surface of blue only
to be peeled back revealing another
surface on which we can't be stable
      though continue the drift
in the lens of imagination
and if it be still of the human past
let it.

13.

On the way always as a returning
       as a surface of blue only
in the distance becomes water
beyond parching
          as life giving
sustenance of the destination
is revealed
though only for this brief pausing
       and not for satiation
which is temporary
respite in the journey
          like me and my mom
like awesomely back there
at the beginning.

14.

Finally upon paper
of past activity or perhaps
       fixed on film and in the memory
above such archeology
          in this heated nostalgia
which is night's hoard and endless
under which another surface
the little plane casting a watermark
       like me and my mom were like inside
but like very painful
though having suffered for the gain
to be peeled back revealing another
as life giving
on the way always as a returning.

Roughly There

Turning back to mark the spot
where she was standing,
        branches having formed
in my absence a canopy
    or ceiling, filtering noon light
to become a kind of evening,
causing me to stumble
at the crest where she went over
and almost
back in her company again,
    I was able to pause, hold on,
and take stock of things.

She was standing there, roughly
where you are now.
    The tragedy, I thought,
that all her fruits should be of labor
and only I left to record them
and her termination.
        Just stepped over . . .
Out in the air only for moments . . .
    A fall, before sudden stop . . .
The story is driven
        in search of a reason.
For the public, chalk it up
to accident.

Where you are now,
a purse tossed in the grass,
    glasses, a scarf blown back
to flutter
on that branch before I retrieved it:
        tangible leavings
to make something of.

The purse was a cloth handbag,
      glasses on the National Health,
the scarf, Armani.
         What did you say, a storm?
     On the cliffs here
there are many, but not that day.

The Princess at work in the keep
counting out coins,
     hammering at the kiosk,
no more leverage.
We had gone dancing the night before
and the child was still stuttering.
      You didn't know of the child, the heir?
His is buried where you are,
roughly there.

[I did know. Hands fingering my hair,
the tale told.]

Dramatic deaths in the telling, the docent,
when the boy came in with the multitudes,
    to learn of his parents,
both fallen from grace in adultery,
the castle haunted
        and now invaded,
tourists touching the dusty fabrics,
looking in to forbidden rooms.

    We lived in the far wing, somewhat
isolated. She kept
the keep and the boy safe, her sister his mother
and the real Princess, riches
        to be handed down at his maturity,

and in the meantime, tourists,
         the admissions kiosk
being built then at the barbican,
this castle the size of a small city.

[And in that city, our assignations,
bodies draped over dust covers
upon opulent furniture
                  below tapestries. My scarf
in use erotically, then given up to her,
Armani, now memento mori.]

Pleased to remember the final night
we danced together,
         no care for coin after the first
flush of invasion. They came in droves,
anxious for tangibles,
         that brush and comb,
table and place setting of the final meal,
his suit worn on that fateful day,
replicas of the knife
and poker the police took away.
         The boy beamed and lost his stutter
temporarily.
I saw him, from where I was often hiding,
behind heavy drapes
and velvet ropes in the drawing room.
         The docent winked at him,
who was coming
to some enlightenment.

[We too went dancing,
         in the unreconstructed ballroom,
ruins of a bandstand,

fractured tables on low risers, ripped away
velvet, and the smell of rancid wax.
                A tape recorder played our tunes softly,
songs of better times,
there in our quarter in the castle city,
cousin. I was the docent, in disguise.]

       She became his mother after the tragedy
of the dead sister I had courted
before our marriage
       and the moving in with them,
she, the boy, and her husband,
all of them drawing me, each in their way
to wickedness,
       and perhaps my Princess
saw this early on,
in dancing . . . glancing . . .
       in the way I'd lost
out to a gold digger pharmacist,
            in my attentions to the lad,
though I'd refused her children
from the very start.
You'll understand all this,
your credentials as a biographer.

[As a docent, I was bringing him
to an understanding,
       fates of the castle made public
in her extremity.
The coins were listed in denominations,
each one squeezed.
       Then there was this other accounting.
In the meantime
rolling around with each other

      in relief of financial anxiety,
and I came to love her.]

Not for love or money
have I come here again with you.
      The scarf reminds me
something else was afoot.
It was Armani
and now locked safe in the keep
as memento mori.
A possibility of some vague retribution?
      She and the boy are dead.
I'm wealthy.
You can write that down, but the other
shall remain, always, a mystery:
      the knife and poker,
the brush and comb,
his pockets
stained by the pharmaceutical chemicals he always carried
and spoke about incessantly. One of them
      suddenly hungry for a meal other than that provided,
though it was pheasant that night,
white truffles
      the boy wouldn't eat, his stomach
and throat twisted
in awareness that something
was quite definitely not right.

      Her hands then
pressed the table in her rising,
having excused herself. She'd passed
the poker in her leaving,
      then came back to stand behind him
before she went.

Maybe he saw my eyes above his head.
      He was gripping the carving knife
and turning.
The boy was watching, his stutter
just beginning.

[My hair in the brush and comb,
      a set of tortoise her sister
had handed down. Is that in the keep too,
wrapped up carefully in the scarf?
The boy saw only the violence.
         As a docent, it was up to me
to provide the history
and cure the stutter. I was curing her
also at that time.
      We came to arrange ourselves
on pews below stained glass renderings
         in the chapel: virgins
and winged children.]

So it's a stand off, I mean
      here we are where she stepped over.
He might have been cuffed across the temple
with the replica poker
         I imagine in mid-stutter
and sudden grief at her leaving. Then,
almost magically, I became the last heir.
      He's roughly there,
almost below your feet.
         It could have been
the branch were the scarf was hanging
and not the poker,
      as he was reaching
out to save her.
You can write that down.

[And write down, too, the end of lives
      in a castle large as a city,
write something about her body,
not for publication,
          the love of a distant cousin.
All retribution
Comes 'round again in a bloody circle
within these castle walls,
the barbican a tower to keep it in.
    "The last one shall be first,"
appropriately,
since we were rolling around
          in a chapel to give her succor,
impossible I learned,
when she had informed me of her plans,
then handed down the potion
    the pharmacist left behind:
to step over . . .
out in the air only for moments . . .]

    She and the boy are dead.
I'm wealthy.
Let us return now for a quiet dinner,
pheasant and white truffles,
in the reconstructed banquet hall.
    The tourists are gone,
the barbican's a guard tower once again.
I've given the servants the night off.
We'll eat by candlelight.
        You can ask questions.
Maybe then
we can do some other things together.

[Only time will tell.]

Two Drunks

So sorry
to have nudged the lapidary cases;
you were a stunner, and after swimming
in bourbon after swimming
      you were momentarily your ankles,
ass over teakettle at the bed side.
Nothing to be gained, actually,
but balance,
for I might have fallen down too
and crushed you in hysterical laughter.
        How romantically lustful
we might have been
that day, even remembered
being decorated:
onyx, opal, diamond, emerald.
It might have taken my breath away.

Lockout

Careful, in my turning of the key
    [separated by a door]
though I was satisfied
to be locked out [after long absence]
there was something in oil
[and old glycerine]
to promise, yet prevent entrance.
    [All that time traveling]
to you beyond thoughts of you
[exotic places]
since I had spent countless hours
    [in towers, fortresses,
foreign tongues] without elsewhere,
thinking of a room behind me
[redecorated] closed
against my arrival as I was before
    [a single bed now, colorful
new fabrics]
banished, even in the locks of this town.
[What, exactly, did you expect?]
Homecoming,
    [the laying down of your head
upon the same pillow] studious
excuses [a welcome mat?],
brotherhood, though you are no sister,
    [if I should remember]
times in the cafe [old songs]
the shadow of your smile
    [responsible]
those adolescent correctives
[heart felt].
The hours, the days, the messengers,
the perfumed letters [mine]
    and the pleasures of learning

[now this]
that I have brought back to reward you
            [for waiting] in a head
longing for that pillow,
        tilted, here at the door. [Take it
and the rest away now.
I have been as bored as wood].

Cairo

Upon conclusion of the light fantastic
    and before the steamer trunk
wound up in Cairo,
there were at least a half dozen women
to consider in imagination
or memory in the small cabin.

Let's see: mother,
Old Aunt Edith, the two evil sisters
    and the younger, sweet one,
then the *Chinoise* triplets, two-thirds,
who had followed
when the bar closed down at twelve;
    they spoke "impeccable" English,
yet liked to be addressed in tandem
this way: C-2 and C-3. That's seven
and not six,
and there was one other.

What transpired:
first, some were sober,
    sweet little sister, mother
and the triplet I might have danced the tango with
for a good part of the evening.
Old Aunt Edith
    lurched about
in surface dreams in her rocker,
influence of brandy?,
and the sisters, in their evil ways,
    were trying to tell one from the other.
Sure, we'd danced the night away,
often cheek to cheek,
    but it was hard to figure identity
in another place.

The evil ones had been dancing too,
always together,
      and I'd had a few turns with little sister.
The three others were wallflowers.
      The band, a little awkward in sea swell,
was called The Cairo Express,
though the boat was heading down the porch steps,
a toy upon imagined rapids,
en route to some benign island near the street.
        And the wallflowers? My mother,
Old Aunt Edith, one of the *Chinoises*.
Is it confusing? I was. What about the other?

Second: "It bubbled up along the curbing,
a simmer; how can this be water? Night Life
      in party hats and condoms,
a toy boat riding a dead rat
and moving
      slowly for the sewers
under street musicians
packing up their saxophones and tubas.
      It was August, no French along the *Seine*,
inside the *Louvre*, the *Beaubourg*,"
all those stupefying place names. Was it
one of the *Chinoises*
who'd said she'd not been there for a while,
or was it a whisper
from the trunk itself,
      a scraping as the porter dragged it
down the hard wood steps,
along the sidewalk and the grass verge
heading for the gutter?

The messenger of mortality forgets the story,
the details, *that* one,
stepping forth from desert dunes
    or down a steep metal stairway, shrouded
in steam at the old train station,
who is ragged
    from journeying, his own story,
and reconstructs the other,
        little doilies cut from cloth
and the antimacassar from Aunt Edith's rocker.
He'd hand them ahead
to the one who has decisions
about public consumption,
    but the chest holding the evidence,
upon camel or in baggage car,
has gone somewhere,
      hijacked or uncoupled,
sent to another destination, a mistake
in itinerary.
It might as well be Cairo.

Close in the cabin and crowded,
the trunk at the bulkhead,
somebody's smoking hemp at the porthole.
    "It's our turn now!":
the evil sisters
in their behaviors, in bad postures,
    hands fumbling in the fabrics of their dresses.
The boat bobs down from the final step,
then steams along the grass verge
approaching the gutter.
A faint knocking at the hatch.

            Old Aunt Edith
lurches awake from dreaming,
"Is that the porter?"
One of the *Chinoises* is yearning
      for the missing C.
Sweet little sister commences to weep.

All along I've been traveling
to a destination,
the trunk to precede me as treasure,
      not to Paris or Cairo, but that gutter.
And when I get there?: transgressive,
in danger,
          embraced at the storm drain
by mother, my little boat
gone down in the flow.

But third: the other,
the interloper, the missing sister,
a *Chinoise* cook,
      those slippery midnight eels
and crispy chicken feet in batter,
          dumplings steaming under silver hoods
on the gueridon. Cuttlefish?,
ancient eggs in aspic,
delectable dominos of uncertainty.
Little sister
      weeps for conventional porridge.
It's morning.
She wants toast, jam and milk.
The evil sisters will eat most anything.
Aunt Edith
      has fallen back into dreaming.
Mother is sleeping.

One of the Cs is ready,
           once again, for dancing, the other
fumbles in somebody's clothing.
In advance of arrival, the trunk is gone,
rich scent of hemp at the porthole.
The bow bumps at the dock's fenders.

Or was it cement at the cracked sidewalk?
The messenger is bleeding out memory.
    "They walked, misdirected
through the Cairo streets, baksheesh, and doors opening
surreptitiously into the dark mosques.
          Then they crossed back over
the highway, a dangerous crossing,
and returned, through the hatch,
to find the cabin empty."
          I might as well have been
the messenger of mortality
myself.

A dangerous crossing:
the steps, the grass verge,
      the sidewalk, the curb. The little boat
bobs in the journey. The gutter
          approaches, a simmer, can this
be water? I lean at the storm drain.
    The sisters are watching,
Old Aunt Edith.
The boat moves and the land doesn't.
Scooped up, then, by mother.

Light as a feather, the memory
    of the boat descending, light
as the future,
the chest holding memories of the past.

        How seldom the rising up of the image
of the lost boat in dream
or imagination of the hours of the child
spent in childhood: that vagueness
    of danger, loss, love, impossible
journeys on steps and concrete,
heading for arrival at rivers, *Seine*,
        Nile, or the simple mid-west gutter
at flood tide after a spring rain.
My blond hair was long
    like a girl's hair
in the photograph, mother in love
with a girl,
herself to begin again,
      to do it over again,
because the chest was lost or empty.
How can I now begrudge her,
my grey hair falling at the crown?

Evening, landlocked,
and the day spent in snoozing.
      Old Aunt Edith and the evil sisters
up and around. Where's mother,
little sister, the two *Chinoises*?
Maybe
we've put the past behind us, dancing,
    fumbling around in clothing,
that odd banquet in the morning hours.
Mother has gone ashore for shopping.
    Little sister is in the casino
playing pachinko. The *Chinoises*
have walked out into the boulevards
to practice French.
The little boat's gone down the drain.

If I am sleeping, if
    I am safe, still, in my bed,
it is because of the journeying,
the messenger of mortality remembering,
though piecemeal.
I was scooped up by mother,
    that dangerous crossing,
who is now shopping only
to return again.

One last time: mother, Old Aunt Edith,
the two evil sisters
    and the little sweetie. Three *Chinoises*,
the dancer, one other, and the cook.
Don't forget the porter,
    though in the end it's no matter
that the trunk is lost forever,
somewhere in Cairo.

Foolish Heart

The blush on memory recalled
still sumptuous
as clerical robes cast aside,
the Soldier of Jesus
        unto the handmaiden,
those buckles and bows so
artfully available,
then said his baby prayers.

Bless us and keep us,
      on his knees at bedside in pajamas,
chin on the coverlet;
        and keep too the lost lovers
in pilgrimage,
though hearts be reluctant to start.

Genevieve, that's a name
      fascination as a lovely tune
sung foolishly into the night's
sensation.
        Is that pose painful?
Could we manage the same
dream combinations
and not be embarrassed by our bodies?

The scene is set for dreaming, knocking
at little doors
as in the Advent calendar:
braces behind
        bruised lips
behind the first one,
then Genevieve, much younger.
A door each day,
      but there's a land
between that's hard to see.

So what, that we were innocent
most usually,
      that will fade and fall apart,
foolish lips eager magic
lost and no longer believed in.

On an evening such as this,
Genevieve, fire starter, ever constant,
      the moon was too close,
white light.
Beware.

2.

Love's at the heart fooled before
      fascination. It isn't
take care, that blush
still sumptuous. So what,
constant moon,
that we were given
      the scene innocent. Beware,
Genevieve, braces to cut lips
eagerly foolish
      hearts on an evening sensation
to spend time, white light
reluctant
of statuesque poses,
night like
      incarnation.
On knees at bedside in pajamas,
clerical robes
      cast from the maiden
beside available chin
      on the coverlet, eager

embarrassment, each day the door
dreamed a fire
of buckles and bows.

3.

Bright future intractable
    little lord given to loss
sung foolishly,
lips eager magic, the kiss
statuary.
Is that pose painful?
Bless us and keep fascination's
    scene set for reluctant pilgrimage.
So what, that we were innocent
chin on the coverlet,
    buckles of reluctant soldier
in pajamas
though hard to see.

On an evening such as this,
constant moon,
it's the Genevieve dream,
    handmaiden
artfully available
at little doors.

Beware white light,
    baby prayers, the blush
on memory constructed
still sumptuous.
    It's a name sensation.
That's time,
my foolish heart.

Standard-17, Some Other Time

Buds popping in the garden
        fed by a recent rain, your hair
fed by "gutsy." All the plants are poking
up on a scale of grey to green.
                Is this the current fashion?
Let's make light of it: my hair
        conditioned by the air
is why I wear a cap
        to watch the lettuce closely,
for it will soon turn bitter
beyond maturity.

Not only
        when something comes to mind
but any time
clouds darken this horizon;
maybe we should move to Florida,
        get a condo and a chair
with soft cushions.
        Some other time.
There seems to be enough left for decisions
called up in the lens,
        though wanting only a little
in this presence now.

A border of flowers, cut carefully
at the edges, beyond which
        the unruly,
paint peeling
and the cracked caulking, so much
to be tending;
        guess I'll water these flowers,
pull a few weeds,
                just ramble along

until you've awakened:
"Good morning" and coffee
  in this blessed pavilion,
the new day
but a token of continuance.

Fire remembered in the eucalyptus,
the ambulance still shuddering at the smell.
  Somebody's moaning early,
a woman in her nightgown in the grass.
Or do I confuse
  the cut corpse of a baby girl,
her incision closed with safety pins,
when I was needfully
in violation, and the doctor too
was pale?

It's in the nature of things,
days seem to be racing,
  comes the time for parting
just when things were starting.

Back down the road at Fairyland
  somebody threw up in the bucket ride,
the cleaning left to the operator.
Let's bring on the sick and injured
in comparison to the dead
some other time.

Old rags in the basement
and a moldy shirt,
  some faded Hawaiian pattern, palms
and a pelican.
   Though I had never been there,

I must have been thin then.
    And that raggedy red towel,
where did that come from?

Haven't done half the things we want to
    and the other half forgotten.
We'll never catch up completely.
Oh, well . . .
    rambling with the roses,
yet to avoid these thorns,
    will decorate the pavilion
any rainy day.

Remembering Santa Fe,
a recent trip to warm our bones,
    though it was cold in the mornings.
Each event's eroding,
    those museums on the hill,
the taste of dinner, twice?,
at the Mucho Gusto.
    I remember you,
but not the words unspoken,
not even the talking,
    though that sand-set silver bracelet
is vivid and still here.
There was something,
quietly said, before we bought it.
Let's be glad
    for what we've had,
though soon forgotten,
just as a late reward turns up
from a gift given without attachments.

      This brooch, that other pin,
this feral music
accurate only in the accounting.
Where has the time all gone to?

The loop of a miniature railway tracking
its figure eight,
      a child's pleasure in repetition,
but she was a baby girl
closed up with safety pins.

A woman in her nightgown in the grass,
gutsy in the wind in pretense
to lift her flowered cape,
      but only a nightgown really;
who would be out so early,
under the fiery eucalyptus trees
in morning dew?
          A dramatic picture,
the feral music,
weeping for a short past,
      a seemingly endless future.
She's held together still
      with safety pins,
the flesh
now unfeeling, but nonetheless.

      Conflation of her brows
into a single line,
cause for alarm or the expression thereof,
      urgency of time left for embracing
only her clothing now, this fabric
cross-handed at her elbows.
          We can never catch up

in emblems
moving only in memory's erosions.
Too many words are still unspoken.
I'll bring roses
into the blessed pavilion.
  Life goes on, or it doesn't,
even on the brink of starting.
Oh, well,
  this day's just beginning
and whatever's
    to come forth from it,
even a ghost story
of a child reassembled,
  life still in these magic fingers
as if passing the oxygen.

Optimal in regard to music,
  whose tunes then would remind us,
a captain or a princess,
a king roaming this property?
    Only a passenger for a while
on the figure eight loop,
though various spurs and dead-ends:
a failed marriage,
  embarrassments and bad company.
I'm thankful for erosion.

What was it we did exactly
in Puerto Rico?
I remember the battlements,
  protection from sea assault
anciently, the coffee,
something about your posture
on a balcony,
not quite captured in the photograph.

It's not the memory that links us,
    even those songs are held isolate,
lyrics to be taken quite seriously
at some time or another.
There's a moon over Miami,
    but I refuse to go there.
Old devil moon, too, in windows
in this blessed pavilion
and so much more
    in the manner of music,
hoofing the light fantastic
to Moonglow, Miller's Mood Indigo,
craziest dream,
even on these heavy feet.

Dampened by morning dew,
    fire eating the oxygen,
her gown's held at the shoulders
with safety pins
    and the baby disassembled
right here:

absent of breath, her skin's perfect
as the Blue Moon, lying there
as we all shall do, no longer sleeping.
    White powder on my gloves, green
at the gills, hesitant
    before reaching out to close her up
with safety pins.

It was simply to make mention
    of the dead and the dead without names,
though she of course had one,
    no time to grow into it

but in thoughts
raggedy as that dew dampened nightgown.

I seem to remember it rained then,
    "to mingle with her cold tears,"
but this was California,
in summer, and that's hardly possible.

    Perhaps it was Arizona
when they set fire
to a dead horse in the mountains,
    that feral scent
of scorched leather, gone up in smoke
like memory,
though I'm sure of the cold morgue
and the safety pins.

I wanted only
    a little rambling, some watering,
a few yanked out weeds;
just passing the time until you awakened
and the blessed pavilion
found its order, on track again in the sun.
    Oh, well, some other time.
There seems to be enough left
to start forgetting.

Feather

Tripping the light fantastic
when the air is so soft.
      Do bugs turn over on their leaves
for snoozing, as I do,
a book open at my heart,
in a lawn-chair
          on this new platform?
"Sturdy," says Larry.
      "It's not going anywhere."
Too sturdy for any foreseeable necessity,
which is my way.

Just a mystery,
      in which a man . . .
two women . . .
a dog as sentinel observer . . .
         Maybe the witty detective
can solve it, then go home.
      The book's now fallen to the platform
at the chair's side.
Maybe I'll wake up again, in rain.
All joy is temporary.

Fantasy baseball?
One might think of a man
      gone sour because youth was
a disappointed trip to the rained out game,
Marilyn's refusal,
         one of a few stinging nettles
still remembered.
He just can't get shed of that one.

The memory longs to forget, blah, blah,
      in this perfect day,

nothing to say.
He went south into Virginia,
        or was it North Carolina?
Was it indeed Marilyn?
    He can't find the itch. Lust, too,
is temporary. When will it get going
finally?

In the mystery,
the man takes a women,
        the dog watches, and the other woman
hears scratching
at the door foreshadowing confrontation.
Is it a guide dog?
    Somebody winds up dead,
and in the reading
I'm glad it isn't me.

        I've been that detective,
not quite as witty,
but in the end I go home too.
    You're just a few feet away,
in the kitchen, cooking up something.

        "What happened?
At the conclusion,
was there a satisfactory solution?"
There's a feather
    on the floor at your feet,
a clue, unaccounted for.
        "Yeah,
but the dog,
it still nettles.
I can't make much out of that."

Hooked

Fish gotta swim, and pheasants
must rise from the fallow corn,
until fish get hooked

and shotgun opens, a crack
in the winter air. Now begineth
the long night, period.

Yet connected to a source of power,
the clumsy ship off the coast
of Ireland, black night's water,

his hand at the tiller and the damaged
hooker on deck between them,
mate and captain, the only crew.

Over the waves, a distant beacon,
foreign hum in the dark engine: a story,
any story.

Table

The table was a tree
before the men and machines
    got hold of it
and made it into something
unrecognizable, erasing its source
in history.

When the tree fell,
it sighed for the lost view
of opportunity,
    that weight in the top branches
in the wind
when the boy climbed
for a look at the outer world, the future,
or perhaps it was the boy sighing.

    There was in fact little to see
of interest to boys,
before girls, who made model airplanes
also with a source in wood.
This was a long time ago,
    when the world was younger.
It's an old piece of furniture.

I sit at the table, thinking possibly
of the tree, the boy, that view,
    all seemingly felt in the wood,
even through
the polyurethane finish
I have provided against stain.

But what is stain, a circle
    of sweat from an iced glass,
spill-over at surfeit,

imprint of the damp palm's signature,
any soaking down
        in search of the living sap,
which is no longer there?

The table is dead, the boy is dead,
    the view will never be seen again
from that exact vantage,
        even though he was probably thinking
of girls with no knowledge or specificity
and not really looking.
I, oddly, am still alive.

And the chair?
What passions do I release in this repose,
palms on the table, a hard chair, so I might avoid drifting
    into dangerous day-dreaming,
and yet I do anyway.

Gloriole, a nimbus
provided by sun through branches
    at the rot of a creek
where crawdads dwelt
and the tadpoles turned into minnows,
now an industrial complex of some sort,
    as much of the Midwest
as well as California
is laid waste.

You might have been Barbara,
or Jean, or Barbara-Jean,
        dope on my fingers
covering that other scent,
not of eucalyptus, that was later,

but the redolent pungency of uncleanliness
in childhood.
      The wood then
was the berry-vine, smoked not for pleasure
but imitation. Perhaps
          the adult can be a child again,
for loss there also was gain.
She took the crawdads home and cooked them,
mother attentive at her elbow.
And now the window.

Looking back up from arthritic knuckles
the wood frame holds,
     as a space through branches,
other trees, birds,
         a blond cat, sky-blue,
and the bay's waters
placid now, almost a mirror
after turmoil
     of storm marking the tail end
of a wintery spring.
New leaves obscure the feeder,
     weeds dip at the planters' lips,
the cat's pregnant.
There are clocks everywhere.

Foolish, then, was our decency,
a naivety considering only tomorrow
     or the next day as future,
a trip to the Pike
for magic of freaks and hot-dogs,
on our bikes, going
     just about anywhere, for comfort
of returning.

The last time I saw you crushes me,
your hands on my shoulders,
  sniffing the foolish bath of perfume,
just the image of you standing there
before falling away, as if
hacked from wood.

There may have been death
all around us. There was,
but we couldn't touch it, that future:
  sap dried up in the cripples,
failed surgeries, heart attacks,
and amputations.
    I remember only your hands
at the frame, looking in a me,
that adult posture
—your mother,
  your father going off to work?—,
but I'm not really trying.
    Wasn't there a eucalyptus tree,
that scent, redolent with death?
  It seems a little sinister now,
but only when I push it.
Perhaps the whole room is a tree,
but for the lamps, bed, and the carpet.

It's a long way from "my home town,"
one of many, and thus
  dozens of gestures of endings
as life goes on without you.

I just wanted to go back once again
for a moment,
but the tree now is a table.

   Only the dead seem stable,
palms pressed down on the surface.
  I can see for a good distance
through the window,
    tall trees in the future
at somebody's horizon
where the sap still resides.

Prayer for Travelers

— for Jean-Pierre & Aline Seeuws

I pray now unto the gods of travel,
who are vessels
containing absence in the mind
and, in the body, anticipations of arrival,
who are gods only
in creation of ambivalence,
and to their witnesses,
      sedentary old men and old
women, who sit on benches in the square
watching comings and goings,
briskly in mornings, heads tilted
earthward at evening's exhausted
returnings
and witnessing those also
      arriving from other places,
this square and the buildings beyond it
a new place, and those leaving
lugging belongings
who will not be returning.

What is home? This square,
      these flowers, annual stink
of the ginkgo, a catch in the throat
at sound of the traveler's footsteps coming
from Houston? Paris?,
      business of busyness,
that dim light in the window
placed there only to welcome him
back again, a homecoming,
though everything seems temporary
in this uncertain America.

Embarrassment of wars and of patriots,
>   agony of children sent to die in places
where the children of those places are also dying,
frustrated rage at politicians
bent on traveling to town squares
for vacuous talking and at those sitting
complacently in offices, plotting
the permanent absence of others.
Where then is home
>   when houses fall down and even
squares disappear while travelers are away?

Let us pray then
in anticipation of this departure
and the arrival which is a homecoming,
as the light left behind is extinguished
along with these voice that say, stay, don't go.
Let the travelers return to the foreign
yet familiar, the stink of ginkgo faint
>   feeling in the nostrils,
that bark on the old trees, the ancient
city squares, the rediscovery
in the unpacking of forgotten belongings.
The scent of remembered flowers,
>   strange in their redolence,
will fade into the common after a day, a week,
until home reclaims them completely
and they can think once again
of those left behind,
in this sweet and uncertain America.

Moon

Oh moon within my vacant gaze,
her figure turning vivid in memory
as if you were modern
and she celebrant of your lost innocence,
no matter they have played golf
upon your bland surface, not of trees,
rivers or pollutants.
She is guileless,
yet attendant to my needs
though I don't often see them.
Oh slice of moon, satellite, green cheese,
I beseech thee,
let this continue indefinitely
under your changing variety of signs.
Since I have found love,
what else is there?
These astronauts
have not really altered the view,
her figure turning, still vivid
under your glow in the memory.
That this could go on forever,
let it.

Gardening

Behind things left in front,
under the faint yellow
light of a nightclub,
as if a drunkard in decay
hidden by fractured neon,
this grapefruit
dressed up for oblivion
in a fur of mold.

What else has been forgotten,
a light in the basement,
anniversary of the many heroes,
some sour appointment?

Having tried unsuccessfully
to keep trying, having
arrived at no understanding,
might have purchased a ticket
to exotic places,
then forgotten the pruning
of acquaintances and closer company.

Yet a blush on the green tomatoes,
the silvery eggplant in maturity
discovered behind leaves.

Clouds open like heavy curtains,
light of the morning sun.
What is ready is cut free.

www.ingramcontent.com/pod-product-compliance
Lightning Source LLC
Chambersburg PA
CBHW031155160426
43193CB00008B/372